SALES DYNAMICS: THE FIRST STEPS

Elisabeth Marino, Founder of
Sales Dynamo LLC

Elisabeth Marino

www.salesdynamoconsulting.com

For my family.

FORWARD

Throughout my career, I've sold, managed, consulted, and spoken publicly, but in my heart I'm always a salesperson. I love being a sales professional! The definition of the job, as I see it, is to learn the goals of your customers, find problems and needs in your customers, and provide solutions to problems that will help them achieve their goals. We solve problems and help achieve goals in exchange for money. We help buyers make the best possible purchasing decision they can. Show your customer that your product or service is worth more to them than the money you're charging for it; that's the tipping point at which your prospective customer commits to owning your product or using your service. As your prospects consider their options, you guide them to the choice that will best suit their goals and needs, and demonstrate that the price is a mere detail that stands between them and the solution we're selling.

I was lucky enough to have some terrific sales professionals in my life teach me the fundamental ropes of the job. As I consult with my sales training clients, I often discover that sales training isn't a part of most salespeople's history! They are taught how to use their company's CRM or sales tracking tools. They're taught how to write up an order correctly. But they have never been taught how to sell! Let's fix that.

Why? Because the internet marketplace has made much of the shopping experience self-serve. It has cost tens of thousands of sales jobs, and it isn't over yet. The only ones who will stay employed in the next ten years and beyond are the ones who add value to their product, company, and clients by being involved in the transaction.

Sales pros are not a dying breed - sales pros are an evolving breed. Become a better sales professional, and you'll be relevant forever.

Sales pros only make money when the rep is in front of the client. An engaging presence and positive interaction skills are vital in every kind of customer interaction. The reason sales pros aren't also the company secretary, or the shop foreman, is because it is a unique, complex, and time intensive job. Sales pros are "always on." We don't have the luxury of having an off day, misspeaking, or making typos. All those things cost somebody credibility, and ultimately, a lot of money. We have to get it right, pop quiz style, every time, and smile while we do it.

A good salesperson is well received by a customer before and after a sale, the first day or ten years later. A good salesperson meets his customer's needs while also meeting the needs of his employer. An expert on their product and their industry, they present the product in the context of the customer's life or business goals. A good sale should be a good memory for everyone involved. A bad experience can be the end of your business.

Shopping for a bouquet, I asked the florist, "How are you today?" as I walked past the counter. She followed me through the shop talking about her personal life until I left. She drove me crazy talking about the problems she was having with her daughter and her landlord. I didn't purchase anything, and I never went back. I didn't want to be the florist's friend, I wanted flowers for my mother-in-law. The business closed within a year.

Sales pros are the face of most businesses, and the reputation of everyone who works for the company depends on them. The best way to maintain or develop a great reputation is to anticipate - and to find ways to meet - a variety of client needs, and make it look seamless. In this book, I focus primarily on outside sales, (a term meaning sales that are made by the sales pro going to the client,) and some inside sales, (the client coming to the sales floor, or is reached by telemarketing.) Most of the concepts work in both scenarios.

Effective salesmanship is a learned group of behaviors. There are folks who are naturally persuasive in conversation. That doesn't mean they possess the skills to find new business, close a sale and maintain a customer relationship. Sales is a combination of technique and creative application of that technique.

What follows are descriptions of important foundational skills, how to build them, and how to implement them. If you want to employ them all, you'll quickly realize you'll need to practice! Incorporate one or two concepts at a time. Sales is a fluid situation. The sales process will continue to evolve as buyers' needs and options to educate themselves grow.

Read the book. Some of the skills will jump out at you as things you haven't tried before. Some things will work well now, and others later. Sales will continue to change. Change along with it, and you'll be in sync with your customers and your manager.

Do you love helping people? Do you want to provide them with the right solution at the right price at the right time? Then keep reading. Becoming the best sales professional you can be is well within reach.

INTRODUCTION

What you can expect from this book

First, congratulations on working on your professional development. You bought this book because you want to be a better, stronger, higher-earning sales professional, and I want to help you do it.

This book is one in a series of Sales Dynamics books, written by me, Elisabeth Marino, founder of Sales Dynamo. I've built my career by helping sales professionals from the newest rep to the business owner create effective skills, strategies, and processes to earn clients and advocates, and by so doing, make a lot of money.

Let me be clear on what this book is not: it's not a handbook to get people to buy stuff they don't want or need. I'm not that kind of sales professional. There are plenty of people out there force-feeding bad choices to people, and they give my chosen profession, sales, a bad name.

This book is more of a field guide – something you can turn to for answers when you're in the trenches. If you're looking for a way to help buyers make the best possible purchasing choice for themselves or their business, then this is the book for you. I see sales as a noble profession. It's something we do for someone, not to them. Helping buyers make the right choice is good for the client, good for my business, and great for my reputation.

There are key components in this book for everyone in sales, from the VP to the newest hire. There are concrete steps, concepts, management responsibilities, and stories that will help you move from your current abilities to a whole new level of skill and earning potential.

Go in with an open mind. Some of these concepts may be new to you, but they are all tested and proven to be successful. You'll see as you read that each step meshes cleanly with those before and after it, creating a cohesive process. If a concept or component doesn't fit with your product or brand message, don't use it, or adapt it to your purpose. But keep reading! The best advice for you may very well be on the next page!

Thank you for buying this book. If you have any questions, suggestions, or comments, I'd love to hear from you. Email me at e.marino@salesdynamoconsulting.com

FOUNDATIONAL SKILLS FOR OUTSTANDING SALES PERFORMANCE

It's not just luck and a smile. – Elisabeth Marino

There is no such thing as a "natural born brain surgeon," although some people are born with an affinity for medicine and neurology. To be a great brain surgeon, you need knowledge and skills, not just a knack. Ditto with sales. There is no "natural born salesman," though some people have a knack for persuasion. The difference between being persuasive and being a sales professional is, you guessed it, knowledge and skills.

These core competencies span every member of the sales team, from rep to manager. How is each skill critical to the success of both the rep and the team? Very! The strongest sales teams are led by managers with all or most of these attributes, and each rep should be developing the skills on this list.

Sales is different from being a clerk. Clerks are a short-term relationship. You don't learn their name, and you don't plan to see them again. It's just a transaction. Sales pros are long-term relationships, and if you're doing it right, like marriages. Okay, we're polygamists, but you get the idea. We establish a relationship to support our customers, and we want our relationship to grow over time.

Each of us probably went into sales for different reasons, but we have several of the same goals as individuals. Each of us wants to make a good living, do something of value, grow our skill set and our professional value, and have a lot of control over what we do and how we do it. Good sales pros make good money. Great sales pros make great money! How do we enter the realms of good and great? We build the skills that will never change in sales, and we hone them to perfection by focusing on them every day.

What is the basis of almost every sale ever made? You may have heard "all people ever buy is pain relief." I disagree. All people buy is a way to achieve a goal. Maybe the goal is pain relief. Maybe the goal is status. Maybe the goal is to have options, or increase productivity, or update their look. Whatever the goal, achievement is what you're selling; no one buys LegosTM because they're bright colors and geometric. People buy LegosTM to have the opportunity to build things. Whatever your customer is buying, you need to provide it to them and take their money. Therefore, every customer's goals are important to you as a sales pro.

What Are Sales Skills?

They are skills and processes that can be trained and practiced that will consistently lead to closed business deals. Understanding what these key proficiencies are and how they contribute to a sales professional's success will allow you to chart your own professional development. As you develop these skills, your numbers will continue to grow.

Sales skills center around three areas: Sales Process, People, and Discipline. We'll review key elements of each area. These are the primary steps to becoming a successful sales professional.

SALES PROCESS

There is no failure except no longer trying. – Elbert Hubbard

How do you go from a prospect to a closed deal? Sales process. Your sales process should be a set of behaviors and questions that take your prospect from being a complete stranger to being a customer advocating for your business in a consistent and thorough way. Your sales process is your prospect's first and primary relationship with your brand – it should be one that creates trust, interest, and urgency. Here are some basic parts of most sales processes.

Prospecting: Reps routinely need to work on finding potential customers to keep the pipeline full. They need to research and uncover relevant industries/demographics and needs, understand market conditions, and define an ideal customer profile.

Introduction: Knowing how to introduce yourself and your offering may sound like a no-brainer – until you realize that almost no one is hoping to be called on by a sales rep today. Understanding how to introduce yourself and generate enough interest to get a meeting is an art and a skill.

Foundational elements include pre-call research, active listening, and knowledge of the prospect's market and business cycle.

Discovery: In sales, discovery is the step in which the sales rep is learning directly from the prospect, and the prospect is learning about the rep's offering. Correctly handled, the prospect learns at their own pace while revealing to the rep the details of what they need. It helps pinpoint the needs of the prospect, and has the prospect stating all the problems their needs are creating, and why it's urgent to solve the issue now. Key to successful discovery is asking the prospect questions and pointing out concerns they haven't thought of yet. This helps confirm your position as an expert who can help the prospect move forward.

Having the prospect tell you exactly what you need to know about pain points and acceptable solutions takes a group of conversation-management skills. You must ask the right questions in the right way, and do so without making the prospect feel pushed around. Once you have the key information, it's important to set a clear expectation of who is taking what next steps, and when.

Proposal: The proposal is the step in which you, the rep, propose a solution. Depending on the situation, you may offer the complete solution as one step, or you may propose the prospect act in a series of steps. Often, the prospect will need the proposal in writing, and it will be discussed by a team of people who aren't meeting with you. (The stakeholders and influencers could include a spouse, partner, or other department heads, among others.)

Writing a concise proposal that tells your story as well as you would takes skills and planning. To be most effective, most sales reps rely on micro-scripting key points to position their offering as the obvious, desirable solution. When you deliver your proposal, your goal is to make an advocate out of whoever receives it from you.

Alignment: The alignment stage is the part of the sale in which you smooth out all the inevitable differences between your ideal sale and the prospect's ideal purchase. Don't rush this step – it can only come after you've made your best recommendation, which can only happen after a thorough discovery. Perhaps they need a different size, delivery schedule, payment plan, or other customization. This step is usually the key to an effective closing conversation. This is when you'll disclose any potentially touchy terms and conditions, and learn to work around their terms.

Making the necessary allowances while not changing your recommendation of the correct solution and maintaining the integrity of your brand are the keys to a successful alignment. You need to deliver the solution you promised while adapting to the prospect's needs as a buyer.

Closing: Closing is the stage where the prospect becomes a customer. It is indicated by the signature on an agreement, or the exchange of money for goods or services. Asking the prospect for the sale is the number one hurdle for sales reps to clear. After all the other steps, it may seem obvious that it's time to close, but most buyers need a little nudge to close the deal.

During and immediately after the close are the most vulnerable points in the sales process. Prospects may decide they've made a mistake (buyer's remorse,) worry they've over-spent, or fear the change to a new provider. Making the closing a high point requires a successful sales process and strong communication skills.

Upselling: Reps need to be able to identify and capitalize on opportunities to extend their relationship with customers. Ideally, over time every customer will become aware of all of your relevant offerings, and their interest will build to a purchase. This requires planning, staging of the sales relationship, and a strong relationship after the first sale is made.

Key attributes for this skill are using an ongoing discovery process even after the initial sale, effective account management, and time management.

Pacing: Different prospects will be ready to move through the sales process at different rates. Knowing how to pace the steps of the process keeps a prospect from feeling overwhelmed by information. You want to educate and guide your prospect at a pace that they can absorb, while maintaining and building a sense of urgency to resolve their issue. Listening skills and time management are key to pacing your sales process correctly.

Selling against the competition: Nearly every sales organization faces competitors. A competitor is any choice a prospect can make that will make them no longer need/want your offering. Being fluent in the positives and negatives of your main competitors' offerings is crucial to helping your prospect make the best buying decision for their situation.

To do this successfully, a rep must have facts when pointing out deficits, and an answer to each of the competitor's assets. Tact is critical, and we cannot directly criticize competitors without looking unprofessional. It requires the rep to have depth of knowledge, already possess the trust of the prospect, and available third-party verification of your evaluation of the competitor's offer.

Time Management: Most of a sales rep's daily activity isn't monitored or directed by someone else. Every day and every action is left up to the rep. Therefore, it is incumbent upon the rep to manage their time and their activities to maximize their results. (More on this in the Time Management Section.)

Key skills to time management include planning, discipline, punctuality, and organization. Without these skills, a rep is destined to end up in hot water with their manager, and sometimes their clients.

Accountability: Due to the independent nature of most sales work, having a strong sense of accountability for your actions is vital to long-term success. Sales professionals who know when and how to ask for help and guidance do well. Those who learn from each deal that does and doesn't close grow their skills quickly. Reps cannot control the behavior of the market, prospect behavior, the weather, fulfillment, or dozens of others of factors. What they can control is how they act and react in these situations. They accept responsibility for their actions, inactions, and failures, which makes their victories even more exciting.

PEOPLE

If I had asked people what they wanted, they would have said, "Faster horses." – Henry Ford

Even in B2B sales, people buy from people. Being able to relate to people and understand their drivers in their buying process makes sales a more pleasant and effective relationship builder. Being able to pinpoint what the buyer needs, not just what they want, builds loyalty and trust. Listening skills, questioning skills, engagement skills, and the ability to effectively guide and manage a conversation all matter in every sale.

Rapport: In sales, we are inevitably asking our prospects to look at their existing pain point or need in a new way. In order to challenge their current assumptions and solution effectively, it's vital that a rep can build a rapport of trust and expertise with the prospect. Understanding how to help a prospect open up to the possibility of change is a foundational skill to sales.

There are many ways to engage with a prospect, but the end goal must always be kept in mind: establish yourself as an expert who is willing to serve their agenda and meet their needs. This is the most direct path to trust and relationship.

A large part of building trust is listening. Speak very little about yourself and your offering in the beginning. Encouraging a prospect to keep talking about relevant information can be accomplished by paying close attention, taking notes, and asking open-ended questions. Never interrupt! Until you fully understand the prospect's situation, there is no way you can confidently offer them a solution.

Emotional regulation: Sales is frustrating. People make bad decisions, withhold key information, make emotional decisions, waste time, break appointments, and more. Understanding that all of this is part of the process and remaining calm and positive can be difficult when you're up against quota. Prospects will ultimately make their own decisions. Unless you've conducted yourself badly, it's not personal. Even if they choose not to buy from you, if you've left a good impression of yourself and your offering, they may advocate for you in the future.

Buyers are people. They prefer to work with people they know, like, and trust. An emotional hurricane is not a charismatic situation. Pleasant and knowledgeable, ready to serve experts are who buyers want to see. You can be friendly, folksy, intellectual, casual, or formal – it's not a personality question. You just need to present a consistently pleasant and knowledgeable personality for your buyers to continue to engage.

People with emotional restraint, who see the upside, and know that they don't need to react to every situation do very well. Pessimists, those who take things personally, and those who lack patience usually do poorly in sales.

Conversation Management: Everyone goes into every sales meeting with an agenda. Making sure that you meet all the points of both your and your prospect's agendas is key to moving through the sales process and making a sale. Letting a prospect pull you off track or run the meeting usually ends in "no sale."

Key skills in this area include asking for the right length of meeting (not too long or short,) keeping the conversation (pleasantly) on track, crafting questions to keep your prospect expanding on what you need to know (discovery,) validating your prospect's concerns and needs, and more.

A meeting that's scheduled for too much time makes the rep look disorganized. So does a meeting that's scheduled for not enough! In my experience, the most popular length of an initial meeting for someone to agree to sit with a sales rep is 20 minutes. It's long enough to justify that there's something to discuss, and short enough to be fit into busy schedules. After the initial meeting, you should have established enough credibility to schedule a longer meeting if needed.

Developing Urgency/Driving the Sale: Sales is about helping people to make the best possible buying decision for their situation, so knowing how to maintain momentum and urgency is essential. Redirecting the prospect to the pain their need is causing and helping them picture a fully resolved future situation are just some of the techniques used to keep things moving.

Important attributes for this skill include confidence in your offering, and the ability uncover and understand the depth of the prospect's need.

DISCIPLINE

Discipline is the difference between what you want now and what you want most. – Unknown

S ales pays well because it's a complex, often difficult job. Frequent rejection, moving deadlines, changing product lines, and literally dozens of skills all converge in a sales rep's workday, and staying out of the weeds takes discipline. Understanding which tasks and attitudes are critical right now while keeping all the balls in the air is part of the daily grind. Most sales reps work with little direct supervision. And with no one holding your feet to the fire, self-discipline is instrumental in consistent success.

Networking with other professionals is often misguided. Networking is not collecting business cards; networking is creating relationships with others who will either advocate for you and your offering, or refer you business, or provide you with information that is important to your market. It can be a rich source of strong referrals, which are the most valuable leads of all. Your network is one of your strongest assets as a rep if you develop and maintain it properly. Making time to remain connected to your network takes planning and discipline. Don't let it get away from you!

Sales managers sometimes overlook the importance of networking in their reps' schedules. If you're a sales manager and you don't see networking on your reps' calendars, remind your reps to work on maintaining their network on a regular basis.

Prospecting is an ongoing task for sales reps, even if you have an appointment setter to help you. Every rep is responsible for a certain amount of new or upsell business, and that means every step that gets you there is your responsibility, too. Prospecting is work that many reps avoid, and their meager pipelines show it.

Sales managers should be coaching their teams to dedicate time, thought, and creativity to prospecting several times per week. Additionally, it is key to remind reps that all prospecting activity should go into the CRM.

Qualifying leads is a vital part of the prospecting and discovery process. Using consistent criteria to qualify and score leads will help you address the most promising leads first, and keep you from wasting time on those who are unlikely to buy. Again, all qualification and scoring data should appear in the CRM.

Here are a few attributes to consider as part your lead scoring system:

Job title or role

Industry

Budget, Authority, Need, and Timeline criteria

Size of company (locations, employees)

Cross-selling opportunities (higher loyalty rate)

Known pain points

What competitor they use

Who made contact, them or you?

Sales managers can save their reps a lot of time and frustration by providing clear qualifying criteria. Make sure your reps understand what factors are deal-breakers, and what makes a prospect attractive.

As the market evolves, make sure your qualification criteria does, too.

Continuous professional development is the most important thing in having a successful sales career. Reading books and blogs, attending conferences and seminars, and making the most of coaching sessions can keep your skills and your perspective fresh. Sales is always evolving. If you're not improving, you're falling behind!

Sales managers should focus on having developmental sales meetings in which they provide reinforcement and development of key skills. Professional development time should be built into the management plan to keep reps engaged and successful. Keeping all skills, even rarely used ones, fresh and sharp will help reps do a better job of representing your brand in the market.

TIME MANAGEMENT

Either you run the day, or the day runs you. – Jim Rohn

What does a sales rep need time management for? Without it, you'll soon be drowning! Let's look at some typical monthly KPIs for an outside B2B sales rep.

50 cold calls (door knocks)

60 referral and sales calls

40 account management calls

12 presentations/closing calls

20 Grip and grins (networking calls)

80 prospecting phone calls

Let's break it down. In a four-week month, 50 cold calls per month is 12.5 a week. 60 referral and sales calls means 15 per week. 40 account management calls is 10 per week. In whole numbers, so far, we're at 37 calls per week. Presentations would be roughly 4 per week. Closing appointments would be 3 per week. Grip and grins are 5 per week. This puts us at a grand total of 49 calls per week. Then we need to add 20 prospecting phone calls per week. We'll look at it now as a

20-workday month. (Most months have 22 workdays, so the numbers leave a little wiggle room.)

Clearly 49 calls per week plus phone calls is going to take some time management! If you hit all the management numbers, you're in front of or on the phone with a prospect or customer just over 84 hours a month based on how long each appointment type takes you to run.

84 hours per month in front of a prospect or customer... 21 hours a week isn't terrible, but it doesn't leave much free time. Why not? That 21 hours doesn't include any prospecting call time, paperwork time, email time, research time, or travel time, which is totally unrealistic. Travel time for an outside rep on an easy day might eat an hour, and on a rough day up to four. Paperwork and CRM time get added in. Preparing quotes and designing presentations eats time, and of course, all the internal company meetings eat time. Making it all fit is an art and a skill.

One of the biggest lessons most new reps learn quickly is, "If it matters, schedule it in your calendar." Winging it may work here and there, but it's usually the fast track to nowhere.

How long do you schedule for each type of call? It depends on your mastery of the material (new products and offerings might take a while longer at first,) but you should know your general average, as calculated above. Clients prefer knowing how long a visit to plan for because they have schedules of their own to meet. If you say, "I need 20 minutes of your time," that's what will be expected. Begin and end on time.

If you don't know how long each appointment type takes you, on average, your schedule will be a mess. Your timing is key to working out a functional schedule. Time each meeting for a few weeks and make notes on how long each type takes. Then you'll have some averaging to do, to see what's the norm. Then you'll have real numbers to work with. Are your calls running significantly longer than your peers? Then it's time for better conversation management. Keep things on topic so your calls will be more focused and shorter.

Not all calls are created equal, so it's important to figure out what calls work best when. In my experience, grip and grin calls don't go over well on Mondays. Neither do cold calls. Everybody is just too busy for a drop-in visit! Monday is a good day to schedule presentations, closing appointments, account management, and referral calls. Friday appointments often get pushed into the next week, so I "schedule" grip and grins and account management blocks of time on Fridays.

I've learned to schedule for the longest I'll allow an appointment to run, because some clients make me wait. (Whether their day got crazy or they planned poorly, I have to sit there...) I schedule longer calls earlier in the day, when everyone is fresher and has a longer attention span. (I also bring the client coffees to early morning appointments!) Shorter calls happen in the mid to late afternoon.

Learn how long your calls take you. Write down a reference for yourself and put it somewhere you can refer to it every time you schedule an appointment until you have it memorized. Within a few weeks it will become automatic, and until then you won't schedule being in two places at once.

To keep my schedule on track, I've decided that account management, cold calls, and grip and grins don't get hard appointments, they get blocks of time like Tu, Wed, and Th from 2-5pm. Account management calls have loose commitments: "I'll be by on Thursday afternoon." This leaves me a little room and flexibility to make cold calls or grip and grins around the address of a presentation call without running late or early to the account management call. This works well in my market. You'll discover patterns of what works in yours. Respect them! It will make for fewer rescheduled appointments.

CONTROL THE CONVERSATION

A conversation is a dialogue, not a monologue. – Truman Capote

One of my favorite pitfalls to discuss in all sales calls is conversational control, because without it your sales career is on shaky ground. How do you feel about someone controlling a conversation? Most people react badly to the phrase. Let me explain all the reasons that it's not just good, but vital that you learn this skill. There are three major problem categories that sales professionals can find themselves in if they don't start with a plan to control the conversation.

Show up and throw up is a memorable term for talking way too much in a sales call. When I'm nervous, it's very easy for me to fall into this category! With all the features and benefits you want to cover, and a clear agenda in your head, you may find yourself droning on, or worse, cutting off your prospect while they are talking. If this is a pitfall you can relate to, it's important to learn conversational control by questioning, and not by talking.

Wallpapered is the term often used for a sales call where the salesperson couldn't get a word in edgewise. There are plenty of buyers out there who love to extoll their knowledge and wisdom, and a sales pro is a fresh audience. Following the "don't interrupt" rule with these prospects can lead to epic failure because there is no time they aren't talking! Breaking in with a gentle, "I'd really like to respond to that" can sometimes turn things around. "I could talk about that all day, but they pay me to talk about _____" will usually get things back on track.

Running late – If you let someone else control the conversation, you may spend 15 minutes listening to the details of their daughter's graduation from college, and how they're doing on the golf course before you can get around to the sale. There are plenty of people who look at having a sales pro in the office as a great time to relax, take a break, and waste time. This is fine for a minute or two, but you need to run on time. You can't just rush the client through the call when they finally run out of breath! You'd be feeding them from a firehose. They'll never remember what you said, and you'll be running late. If you can't control the conversation, there is no way to ensure you stay on schedule.

Instead of winding up in the situations mentioned above, we manage the conversation. Sales professionals work to be excellent assessors of need. We ask the right questions to qualify and identify needs in every prospect we meet. We make sure all the right information is covered. We ask the right questions, and listen carefully to the answers.

Think about going to the doctor's office. The sales process is like the process a doctor goes through. The doctor examines you, the patient. He asks you a variety of questions to make sure he understands your complaint, your concerns, and your needs. If you go in for abdominal pain, you may not know that your dry itchy skin could be a symptom of the same ailment. Your doctor needs to ask the right questions to make the right diagnosis. Likewise, you need to ask the right questions to establish the prospect's needs and goals. Listening and questioning are what make the visit work for both sides.

When I tell salespeople to control the conversation, many of them grow uncomfortable. They picture pushy, fast-talking doublespeak. No one wants to be sold, and we all know it! Remember the doctor-patient example. The customer doesn't know what they don't know. If your product is fire-retardant, comes with Bluetooth capacity, or is completely made in the USA, they probably won't discover it until you bring it to their attention. You are the expert on your products. Controlling the sales call allows you to learn their needs, reveal information about your product, and gain qualifying and purchasing information from your shopper. Controlling it well will keep your customer happy and engaged.

12 Points of Controlling the Conversation

The brass tacks of controlling a conversation come down to 12 points. They are simple to list, but take a little practice to master. Don't worry! Each one leads naturally into the next, reminding you of where you're headed. These techniques are effective in person and on the phone. Practice each one for a full day. You'll be a better salesperson in 12 workdays. Here they are:

1. **Write it down.** Write down your agenda points. Write down your basic pre-call research. Write down what they would like to add to the agenda. Write down what they say. The better your notes are, the better able you will be to manage the conversation in a way that keeps the prospect engaged.

2. **Start with a smile and a warm greeting.** You know the smile you give when you unexpectedly see a dear friend? That's the smile to share with your prospect the moment you make eye contact, before either of you have said a word. You're setting the tone for the entire interaction. (You can even tell if someone on the phone or radio is smiling when they talk!) How do you feel when you receive that smile? It's the same relaxation you experience when you are welcomed and respected. Give that smile, and mean it.

Whether you've met the prospect before or not, always

greet your prospective customer warmly. (Even if they are mean or annoying!) Greeting your prospect in a welcoming way establishes control, or home court advantage. No one ever welcomes someone in when they're feeling insecure or threatened, do they? Show them how glad you are to meet with them. You're demonstrating that your interaction will be a positive experience. Humans tend toward reciprocity. This means people usually respond in kind to the way they are treated. If they're treated pleasantly, they'll tend to react in a pleasant and agreeable way. Just make sure you're the one setting the tone, and maintain it.

3. **Call every prospective customer by name.** People feel more important when called by name. If you don't know their name up front, shake their hand, introduce yourself, and ask them. Repeat their name once you have it. "It's great to meet you, Mr. Foster. Thank you for meeting with me today." When you need to address Mr. Foster, use his name once every 2-3 minutes. It keeps him engaged, and keeps you from forgetting it! If you believe his attention may be drifting, call him by name in your next sentence or question.

4. **Listen and mirror.** Listen to your prospective customer. Listen to their words, their tone of voice, and their style of expression. If they are speaking quickly and gesturing with their hands, they are probably excited. Mirror a slightly calmer version of that behavior. Likewise, if they are speaking slowly and deliberately, be sure to enunciate and speak at a slower pace. Don't copy their voice or hand gestures exactly. (That annoys people!) Mirroring is a deeper, more active form of listening. These mirroring techniques have been shown to make people feel understood and respected, even when no words are spoken.

What do you get out of this? Mirror the body language of the prospect for a few moments. Putting your body in the some of the same postures they use will help you understand their mood and attitude. If your customer has a slumping posture, slouch just a little, and see how it makes you feel. Are their arms crossed tightly across their body? Cross yours loosely, and see how it feels. Once you correctly perceive their mood and attitude, you'll address their questions more effectively. Learning about your product will be a much more comfortable process for the client.

5. **Talk about your client's situation in their own words.** How does this fit into controlling the conversation? The only context that matters to your client is how to meet his own needs, achieve his own goals, and solve his own problems. Most people prefer to talk about themselves. Encourage them to talk by using probing questions. As they talk, you'll be learning about what product to sell them, why, and often how. Everything they share tells you something about their needs, their qualifications, and about their buying process. Do not interrupt.

Ask them to put things in their own words. Are they constantly fielding phone calls while they're trying to meet with you? Ask if this is a usual day, or if they're especially busy today. You're learning about their stresses, and their needs. What are their short and long-term goals? Use their own words back to them. Naturally you want to encourage them to focus on subjects related to the sales process, but you can link the personal and professional. This buyer is now the primary context for your product. Some of what they tell you will give insight into their budget, or where they've already been shopping. It's good stuff. Apply what you're hearing. "Well, as busy as you are, I'm sure you want to do this efficiently. What questions do you have for me?"

6. **Thou shalt not speak ill of the competition.** Never, ever, ever. Putting someone else down doesn't make your product or company look any better, it just makes you look petty and like a gossip. It's unprofessional. In many

companies, it will get you fired. Most importantly, you are not talking about your product or your customer! Bring your attention back to where it belongs. You can emphasize that your product wears longer, or that your service is backed with a guarantee. "You can make this purchase with peace of mind. We're proud of our guarantee. It's the longest and most complete in the industry."

When your prospect talks about the competitor's product, or a shopping experience they had somewhere else, listen and learn. If they tell an unhappy or frustrated story, empathize and move on to the information you need. "I'm sorry to hear that." Or, "I understand that must have been frustrating. What about that didn't work for you, exactly?" Then, "Let's work on getting you what you need." Don't dwell on the failures of the competition, just respectfully shift gears. You need to understand their need, or problem, and how the competition failed to meet it.

7. **When your shopper finishes a thought or asks a question, move on to the next concept or question you want them to address.** This is the most important skill in conversational control, and it takes a lot of practice to do it smoothly. You may want them to expand on what they said, or respond to a question. But you must be in control of where the conversation goes.

You can do the **three-step**: Ex: Buyer; "and that's why I'm in the market for a new system."

Short pause. "Mr. Client, we have a large selection of systems that will meet your needs. Tell me about how your staff uses the system. What do they need the system to do more effectively?" In three sentences you've responded appropriately, you're in control, and you're learning what you need to know.

Back to Mr. Client: "Well, it would help of they never had to enter information more than once. If the system could scrape data

Elisabeth Marino

from several different applications and generate reports, that would be ideal."

Short pause. Now you: "Think of how much time that would save! We have solutions that do just that. How many staff members will be working on this system?" Again, in three sentences an appropriate response is tied to the next probing question. (And we added the "time save" benefit to address client goals!)

You can also use **support and add**: No matter what the client has said, you'll find a way to be supportive of that, and then build on it.

You: "You raise a great point. We've found that solution B is responsive to that need, and I think it will work for you. Do you need direct control, or remote functionality?" You'll respond to them in a supportive way, and then build on it.

Another use of support and add would be:

Client: "So we could finance this and break it up into 6 payments?"

You: "You sure can. No financial pain, and you enjoy your new floors right away. Did you want smoked hickory, or the weathered oak?" Agree with the client, and then move forward.

As a last resort, there is the **friendly exclamation**. There are all kinds of interjections that stop a speaker from talking for a moment, allowing you to get the conversation back on track. They tend to be said emphatically, and tend to be a single word: wow, no, stop, listen, amazing, terrific, and great. Anything you can interject with a smile to make them pause so you can speak without talking over them falls into this category.

Client: "And so we're planning to hold the party at the country club after all."

You: "Wow! Coincidences like that are amazing. But back to your needs on this project for a minute... Were you saying that the whole team will be using the solution, or just the management group?"

These techniques should be employed on most or all occasions that you speak in the sales process. It makes you efficient, responsive, and most importantly, keeps your prospect talking. Conversational control often fails if you have not mastered these skills.

8. **Praise/thank your prospect**. There is always a sincere reason to praise them, and it shows them you think they are important. "It's a pleasure to meet you." "Thank you for seeing me today."

If you're familiar with their business, say so. "My family has been using your company for years." Even when they call you, work it in. "It's good to hear from you. What can I do for you?" Being gracious works toward your "home turf advantage" positioning. You always want them to feel as if their time and attention was valued.

Your client is, and should feel like, the most important thing you have going on right now. You don't need to grovel, but you must establish interest and respect. Why? Have you ever come across one of those salespeople who treat prospects like they're an interruption or an annoyance? Giving the impression you find your agenda more important than you find your client is a sure way to see to it they don't "bother" you again.

9. **Be well and fine and happy.** Sales is a customer focused activity. If they ask how you are, you're fine, or great or terrific. Now turn the focus back to your shopper. No one cares if your feet hurt, if you broke up with your sweetheart, or if you're in a lousy mood. Well, at least, your client doesn't. Conversation management relies on you to be focused on learning and meeting the client's needs, not yours. Never give them a reason to tune out! Clients want service. Pleasant service. Make sure they

get it.

The good news is we all have breaks in our workday. If you need to vent your frustrations, or take an aspirin, or change your shoes, do it on a break. And if you are one of those who likes to skip their breaks, seriously consider taking them. Having some water, knowing that soon a restroom break is coming up, and just stretching your legs all keep you fresh during your interactions with your prospects. Sales is intense. Breaks make it easier to focus on your clients and their needs.

10. **Try to avoid saying "NO."** It annoys people! Your shopper sometimes will ask you for things you can't deliver. It happens to all of us. If they ask, "Can you give me another 20% off?" You say, "What we can do for you is this -." When they say they want lifetime service free of charge, you can say, "We handle service this way -." Addressing the question with the available choices is usually enough to bring the customer back to discussing the possible. If the shopper presses the issue, repeat yourself.

If you are forced to deny a specific request, be gentle but clear: "We don't offer that option. We're happy to offer this." Sometimes "no" is inevitable, but it is always a last resort. If you have to say it, don't leave it hanging in the air like a bug you want to swat! Follow it up immediately with the solution you do offer.

11. **Create a "Yes" frame of mind.** In your discussion with your client, ask questions which lend themselves to "yes" answers. "You appreciate a good value, don't you?" Or, "Your family is the priority here, right?"

Follow these questions up with immediate facts that serve the subject. "This insurance policy protects your family in the case of a tragedy, and also creates an investment tool to make the good times even better." Once a person sees that you're on the same wavelength, they relax some of their defenses.

Feeling understood helps people build relationships. Prospects stop resisting and start problem solving, which means buying. Several "yes" answers in a row are a good on-ramp to a closing.

12. **"You told me" are the three strongest words you can use in a sales or closing call.** As you're taking notes, you'll be asking the client to put things into their own words. "How long have you been aware of this issue/need?" "How many other processes are negatively affected by putting off a purchase?" The answers to these and other discovery questions become objection-busting phrases.

"You told me you've been aware of this problem for 3 months, right? And you said it affects about 12 people every day? And now you're ready to get those 12 people back to full productivity, aren't you? Here's how I think we should move forward."

You're telling them their own story in their own words, and providing the answer they said they wanted. It demonstrates respect, interest, partnership, and professionalism when you present your business case in the prospect's own words. And you haven't given them a "sales pitch!"

PROSPECTING BEST PRACTICES

Prospecting: Finding the person with the need you can fill. – Elisabeth Marino

Prospecting is a term for activities that help reps identify specific potential customers. It includes collecting relevant details like contact names, phone numbers and addresses, and creating entries in the CRM for each. Use the tagging feature in your CRM to identify certain key criteria, like date, industry, geographic area, lead source, or others relevant to your qualification and sales process.

Prospecting is an ongoing task for sales reps, even if you have an appointment setter to help you. Every rep is responsible for a certain amount of new or upsell business, and that means every step that gets you there is your responsibility, too. Prospecting is work that many reps avoid, and their meager pipelines show it.

Sales managers should be coaching their teams to dedicate time, thought, and creativity to prospecting several times per week. Additionally, it is key to remind reps that all prospecting activity should go into the CRM.

Start with an Ideal Customer Profile

At the heart of every great prospecting strategy is knowing exactly who your ideal customer is, and why.

A common mistake is that reps treat prospecting as if it's strictly a numbers game. They'll target anybody - without knowing whether that lead is a worthwhile prospect. While reaching out to a variety of leads is important, keep in mind that the purpose is two-fold: open a dialogue, and qualify whether they are a potential customer now, or in the future.

Research consistently finds top sellers take the time to understand who their ideal customer is. By doing so they're able to focus on quality over quantity. ICP will help you choose what industries to look for, what clubs and civic groups to network in, and how to quickly qualify a lead.

In some companies you may have different ICPs for different seasons, different products, or different industries. Investigate which clients may be seasonal, and mark your calendar accordingly.

Research Your Lead

Gathering names and contact details of potential prospects is easy. It's when you start digging a little deeper that you determine whether a prospect is worth contacting. Your goal is to create a basic overview of the prospect.

First, check if the lead is already a customer. If not, start your research with a visit to their website. Also, check for any recent news items about them.

Social media is another good data source. Twitter and LinkedIn are typically your best bets because users tend to make their profiles, and their posts, public. See if there's any news about your contact or their team. It's a great ice-breaker.

Limit Research Time

It's easy to get carried away when prospecting – especially when we think we have a strong lead. Sure, the more you know about a prospect, the better – but at the prospect stage, educating yourself on everything about the prospect isn't necessary or realistic. If they are open to an appointment, you can do more research at that point.

Set a time limit for each prospect and stick to it. Once that time's up, you should have enough information to determine whether someone's worth contacting. 5-10 minutes should be plenty. You can always add more info. But if it's a dud, you'll never get that time back.

Assign A Score to Each Prospect

Personalization is essential to cold outreach, but we can't research every contact to the same degree. Beyond a few basic pieces of information, what do you need to know? To help you decide how much time and effort you should put into a lead, score your prospects.

Prospect scoring is the process of assigning scores to prospects based on how likely you think they are to convert. Use these scores to help determine how much time to put into research before the initial contact.

There are no set rules for this. Each rep has a unique presence and personality, and finds different leads easier to approach than others (farms, law firms, manufacturers). Your scores will be different from your colleagues. How do you get started?

Here are a few attributes to consider as part your lead scoring system:

Job title or role

Industry

Budget, Authority, Need, and Timeline criteria

Size of company (locations, employees)

Cross-selling opportunities (higher loyalty rate)

Known pain points

What competitor they use

Who made contact, them or you?

Timing Matters

Let's say that when researching a prospect, you discover that they or their company recently celebrated a big accomplishment. Leverage this to personalize your approach, and reach out as soon as possible! News and social media can provide many of these opportunities.

Numerous studies have concluded that the best day of the week to send an email is Tuesday, and the best day to prospect by phone is Thursday. Door knocks do well all day on Tuesday, Wednesday, and Thursday, and Friday afternoon. (CSO Insights 2019)

Be aware of other timing triggers that may make a difference. Some businesses are sensitive to the time of day, or day of the week (like restaurants and entertainment venues.) The end of the quarter or the start of a new fiscal year may matter.

Ask for Referrals

There's no stronger prospect than one that's generated through a referral. They are 10x more likely to close than cold prospects, and have a longer length of relationship. One study showed referral customers yield a 25% higher average margin. The Harvard Business Review (HBR) found 84% of buyers begin the buying process with a referral.

91% of customers say they'd be willing to give referrals. Sales professionals who ask for referrals earn much more than those who don't. Sadly, only 11% of salespeople are asking. (HBR)

After every sale, ask the customer for referrals. Ask a specific question, like, "Do you have a friend I should be helping?" Asking them if they know "anybody" is too broad, and leads nowhere. Ask again 3 months out – they've had a chance to get to know your product and your service better.

Network

How often do you spend time networking? Get out there! Network contacts are a great resource for warm leads.

Don't expect networking to fill your cup immediately. You need to make lots of contacts and develop a personal relationship with as many as possible. It takes time. Like a sales relationship, you'll lead with value. You'll make a genuine effort to help your network partners achieve success. Networking develops your personal reputation within the professional community, and you'll reap benefits for your entire career.

Prospect Often

Surprisingly, average and top reps spend similar amounts of time prospecting. (Reps who perform under goal spend the least time prospecting, by far.) What separates average reps from the top performers is how they allocate their prospecting time. (Hubspot)

Top performers spend the same amount of time prospecting on the first day of the month as on the last day. (Statistically, buyers are more likely to purchase at the start of the month.) In fact, high performers prospect every day, which keeps their calendars full. (Inc.)

By prospecting daily, their skills never get stale. They spend a little less total time prospecting than the average reps, and their pipeline is always full.

Book time for prospecting every day or at least several days per week – on your calendar – and keep the appointments. Prospect at different times of day; some people aren't available first thing in the morning, last thing in the afternoon, etc. And mix it up. Calls, door knocks, emails, and social media can all play important roles.

Have a Clear Purpose

All outreach needs a clear purpose. Before you do anything else, make sure you can answer the question "What am I hoping to get out of this contact?" Use an "I'm calling (reaching out) because…" statement. No reason for calling means no prospect engagement.

Ex: "Hi! This is Elisabeth Marino from Sales Dynamo. I'm calling because I'd like to have coffee with you and learn more about you and your business."

"Learning more" is a valid reason for contact – make it clear to your prospect that's all you're trying to do. Take the lead. Tell them what you want to happen next. Asking the prospect to dictate the next step will almost always fail.

Use the Phone

Phone calls take most of the wasted time out of the outreach process. No travel, no waiting for a return email, and no need to memorize your research notes – just read 'em! What's not to like? Phone calls should be the largest percentage of your initial outreach.

I know, you may love to text – lots of us do. But unless you know that texting is a prospect's preferred method of contact, don't do it! Some people find it invasive; others simply don't check their cell during their workday. Until you know for sure, assume texting is a bad idea.

Beyond making calls, top reps direct their conversations. They keep the call short and focused on the desired outcome.

Top reps rely on basic research on each prospect to ensure they successfully engage them. They end the call when their purpose has been achieved, and don't try to rush the sales process.

Overcome the frustration and fear of calling by preparing for each call. Create an outline of what you want to say. Then call with confidence. You represent a great offering!

Follow Up

Many reps don't like following up. Or, at least, that's what the statistics say. In fact, 70% of prospects called (called on, emailed) are never approached again. (Salesforce) Yet, we know it takes 5-15 contacts to engage a prospect!

Elisabeth Marino

Use your notes to come up with a second (or third, or fourth) "I'm calling you because…" NEVER say "I'm just following up." If they've already put you on the back burner, "following up" isn't going to get their attention!

Follow up at different times of day, and by different media. Email, LinkedIn, and door knocks mix it up a bit, and keep you top of mind. Keep at it. 5 to 15 follow-ups are pretty standard to achieve an engagement with your prospect.

GENERATING NEW BUSINESS

Indifference and neglect often do much more damage than outright dislike. - J.K. Rowling, <u>Harry Potter and the Order of the Phoenix</u>

For many companies, generating new business is the primary reason the sales force exists. Repeat business is assigned to Customer Service. It's much easier to keep a customer, and cultivate more business with them, than it is to generate new business. New business takes time, and research, and patience, and a high frustration tolerance. Prospects say "no" because it's easy, to save time, because they are intolerant of change risk, and dozens of other reasons. Getting to yes takes skills and perseverance.

New business is a numbers game, too. You'll be calling on lots of folks who aren't ready to buy. Keeping the prospects who reject your offerings looking forward to seeing you again is a big part of the job. You need to become a trusted colleague before you can become their preferred vendor. Most of us work in finite markets. Over time, we may call on a person or business a dozen times or more. If you scare them or annoy them on a visit, you may have closed that door forever. The conversational control tools you learned earlier keep the tone pleasant, and client focused.

There are eight steps to the cycle of generating new business:

Prospecting, Networking, Setting Appointments, Identifying Needs (Discovery,) Building Value, Overcoming Objections, Closing, and Follow Up. You might think it makes sense to start with prospecting, and to an extent, you're right. But prospecting only works if you have a clear, direct message. Here and in the next few chapters we'll focus on what to say.

Building Your Dynamic New Business Plan

I hate the word "Pitch" because the implication is that you're just presenting, without engaging the customer. Not so! Your New Business Pitch needs to have a plan, but not a script. In some cases, your pitch will have some language you use verbatim in every sale. Sometimes there really is only one "best" way to describe things. But generally, you'll conduct every sales call differently, and have an outline of what needs to be covered.

Behaving as a human being (not a computer) is where sales pros excel. Strong outlines and agendas for New Business calls are very effective. Rote-memorized scripts are not. What follows are skills and dynamics to add into your outlines and agendas. You'll stay in control of the conversation, and use these tools to educate, excite, and close your prospect.

Start building an Outline. (You'll run through a few notes and rough drafts as you complete the following exercises.) You'll use this list as a resource to build individual call plans. I keep my individual call plan attached to the clipboard I use to take notes. I refer to it all the time to make sure I cover all the points I intended.

Each heading below should prompt you to add specific concepts, questions, or phrases to your outline. From there you can build an agenda of how you'd like individual New Business and Prospecting calls to run, and polish some lines for maximum impact. From prospecting to follow-up, a consistent, clear message is important. Particularly in the initial contacts, you have very little time to make your case before your potential customer tunes you out. You need to get it right the first time, so you want to have a few lines that deliver your message very clearly, in an inviting way.

Bosses and managers will tell you to discuss features, benefits, and differential advantages. Then what? Do they tell you how? Or when? Features and benefits are easy to find in a little bit of online research, so your prospects can find them in a few seconds from their phone. They are no longer the strongest part of any pitch. You still need to know them, but they aren't your primary focus. Since that's where you manager will tell you to start, we'll start there. Sketch them out, and how they relate to each other, right on your pitch outline. Eventually, they will be built into your finished pitch as individual modules.

Feature – A feature of a product is something positive and observable or concrete. It will include something that sets your product apart, like "leather seats" or "lightweight."

Benefit – A benefit is the way in which the customer's situation is improved by the product. "Added comfort" or "time-saving" are benefits. They define experiences, not something concrete.

Differential Advantage – The differential advantage is the reason your product is the right choice for your customer, as opposed to other alternatives. Differential advantage is usually discussed with features and benefits.

> When it comes to rain gear, most of us would like to stay dry, with style and durability for our money. When we're at Niagara Falls and getting hit with spray from the falls, the flimsy little plastic pullovers at the merchandise stands have the differential advantages of being on site, and inexpensive.

When we deliver a feature and follow it up with a benefit, we can easily fall into a droning pitch. Instead, we want to get the client talking. Clients want to talk about themselves. When we start with a benefit, "Our customers hire us so they don't have to be experts in small business banking," it's easier to stay client focused. You'll follow up with the features in a moment. "How much time do you want your people to spend managing your banking needs?" Listen to the answer. The client will tell you where he wants his staff focusing their attention.

Now incorporate those answers into a client-focused, targeted outline of the features your product/service offers. "Introducing a new product line in your company is what you excel at. We would be happy to manage your payroll and credit card processing for you (features). That's what we excel at. We'll save you time, money, and most importantly, take away that distraction from what you're in business to do (benefits)." These four sentences cover features, benefits, and achievement of the client's goals.

Your differential advantages are usually features, so introduce them to the conversation from the benefit point of view. Again, we don't want to "tell" the prospect. We want to keep them talking. "We know you'll appreciate the immediate response only a local company can provide," is the type of phrase you can work into most of your responses. These differential advantages should be introduced simply, so your client can easily remember them. Jot a few down now, along with questions that will pave the way to revealing those advantages.

Micro-Script Labels

Having a great conversation with someone is much more useful as a sales rep if that person can remember what you said. The more they remember, the better they will do in telling your story to others. Enter Micro-scripts.

Micro-scripts are highly memorable phrases of 2 to 8 words that capture an entire idea in the mind of your buyer. (Like Nike's classic "Just Do It," which evokes the energy and momentum of an athletic event in just three words.) Using them makes it more likely that the prospect will remember key points from your meeting.

Micro-script labels are going to become some of your modules or touch points in your new business efforts. Label them for their benefit or advantage: "responsive-local," "durable quality," "private and secure," or any other pairing. They may not all be very catchy, but they should all be memorable. When the conversation turns to these subjects, you'll have a few pointed sentences ready to keep the conversation focused on how you can support reaching the client's goals. Now type them up and make the micro-scripts you've just made into a list.

In my experience, having a list of 15-20 micro-scripts or so is a great foundation. (Invisible features, benefits, and advantages should also be on the list: ex: 24-hour customer service, 50 years in the industry.) For a cold call or new business call, you'll need to touch on at least 5 points, unified around a theme with three points or fewer, to create a lasting impression in your shopper's mind. Pair that with some terrific discovery questions and some attentive listening, and you've made a lasting impression.

SETTING APPOINTMENTS

Someone giving you their time and attention is giving you a precious gift. – Dalai Lama

When you've prepared for your prospecting call (see Prospecting, the previous chapter) it's time to start setting appointments. An appointment is an opportunity to learn more about a prospect in a face to face meeting. It is not the time to talk about yourself! (Not until they ask, anyway...)

Knowing what you want to say is half the battle. Saying it to the right person in a way that you land an appointment is the second half. The rules are basically the same whether you're speaking to someone in person, or over the phone. (I don't recommend asking for an appointment over email unless it is for lunch, coffee, drinks, or golf.)

Usually when we ask for an appointment, we are interrupting people who are busy doing something else. Because of this, it's important that we don't try to conduct the sales call on the appointment-setting call. Our prospect is unlikely to give us their full attention, or have time to go through a thorough discovery. When you're setting an appointment, that's all you're doing. Set the appointment, and let them get back to their day.

Let's cover some dos and don'ts:

Do use your first and last name (Unless you're Madonna, or Ke$ha, grown-ups use two names.)

Do state the business you're calling from

Do say "I need to speak with 'X'" (not "can I" or "may I")

When connected to the right person, do use your first and last name, company name, and a simple "I'm calling you because" statement

Do come right to the point

Do ask for a specific amount of time on a specific day (not "do you have any time this week?")

Do confirm their best phone and email contact info

Do thank them for making the appointment

Do immediately send them a calendar invite to confirm the meeting

Do answer, "Can you tell me what this is about?" with a short, "I'd like to discuss an opportunity to do business together" or other simple statement. Do not go into the weeds about your company or your offering!

Don't mumble or speak too softly to be heard

Don't call without your pre-call notes in front of you

Don't ask permission to talk to someone (Is it okay if I talk to Mr. Jefferson?)

Don't ask for an appointment over voice mail

Don't type or make other noise while you're on the phone

Don't forget to log the call in the CRM, even if you don't reach anyone

Don't sell on this call (at all!)

This seems like a pretty straightforward and simple list. It is! Selling on an appointment setting call is like dropping your popcorn in the lobby of the theater. It's out of sequence – the popcorn should be gone at the end of the movie. Doing things out of sequence makes some things very ineffective. The main reason reps have trouble setting appointments is they overthink it, trying to cram to much into that call. They try to sell! The other big reason reps have trouble is that they do a lousy job of scrubbing their prospecting list.

The fact is this: if you don't sincerely believe that every single prospect on your list has decent potential to become closed business, they aren't really prospects! Hold every one of your prospects to this standard. There is no point in wasting time on calls that have no chance of making you successful. It may seem scary at first to cut your prospect list this way, but you'll waste a lot less time, and suffer a lot less aggravation.

DISCOVERY

"The seeker embarks on a journey to find what he wants and discovers, along the way, what he needs." — *Wally Lamb, The Hour I First Believed*

The discovery step is the most important step in any sale, whether it's new business or upselling, retail or business to business. Discovery, the learning stage, is what sets a good sales rep apart from a clerk or a vending machine. In the discovery stage, we are learning about our buyer. We are experts in our field, and the buyer doesn't know that they don't know everything. It is our job to help them make the best possible buying decision to meet their needs, budget, and timeline.

Of course, most buyers don't see it that way. They see sales reps as necessary evils – a toll they have to endure to get what they want. The only way to avoid being perceived this way is to add value from the very beginning of the sales call. You must establish yourself as a knowledgeable and benevolent resource early in the conversation to be considered worth the hassle of meeting with you. Like the Wally Lamb quote above, they are looking for what they want, and you must assure them you can help them get what they want and need.

One of the quickest and most effective ways to do that is to ask them a discovery question they haven't thought of yet. Challenge an assumption they have made, and show them that there are alternatives. Disrupt their thinking a little bit. Now you have their full attention.

Discovery Questions

To fully understand what products and services your client needs, you need to learn about the issue that put them in the market. You need to ask some probing questions. Why are you in the market today? What isn't working? Why doesn't it work? How does that affect things? What are the long- and short-term goals? These questions are all about establishing the specific needs of your customer, and bringing those needs to the front of your mind and theirs. Their answers will allow you to identify exactly what advantages and benefits will be part of the solution.

It is very important that you ask questions that encourage the buyer to provide a complete picture of the need. How and when did they discover the need? What solutions have they tried so far? What else are they considering? As you read this section, jot down questions that you always need answers to. Over time, polish the questions to yield the most information while focusing on your prospect's pain and building their urgency to meet goals.

Make notes of your buyers' answers. Not only will you remember their answers, your client will feel respected because you took the time and effort to make notes. Later, when you summarize, you'll be able to demonstrate understanding of the client's goals and needs.

What is a discovery question? A discovery question usually is an open-ended question; a question that can only be answered with an explanation. Some effective discovery questions include:

What has you in the market?

What is/are you/your organization working toward in the short term?

What are you working toward in the long term?

What outcome are you looking for by making this purchase?

How do you use the product or process you have? How would you prefer to use it in the future?

When did your current need arise?

What are the effects of having this need unmet? What is the ongoing cost?

What will be the result of putting this solution in place?

What will be the savings or profit gained by putting a solution in place?

Who is affected by your purchase or decision?

Who else is involved in making this decision?

What is your current solution or work-around?

What isn't working well in your current solution?

In how many locations do you need a solution?

Where do you currently take delivery? Would another location be more convenient?

When do want your new solution in place? What is the rest of the timeline?

What lead you to choose their current solution, and what changed?

How would you like to move forward?

How often does this need arise?

What other needs do you have coming up soon?

These 20 questions represent a partial list of the questions I use on a regular basis. Different products, services, and industries lend themselves to different probing questions. As you work your way through this chapter, develop a list of at least 20 that apply to your situation. Make sure they include questions about goals, who, what, where, when, how, and how often.

Each of these questions is designed to encourage the prospect to tell you everything you need to know to sell them. You can use their own words as you describe the perceived issue, and as you offer the solution. "You told me you became aware of this issue in March. You said you've tried the competitor's solution. And now you're in the market again. What did you find lacking in your current solution?"

"You told me" are the words that show your prospect you were paying attention, understand their issue, and took accurate notes. And it makes it difficult for the prospect to offer meaningful objections when you use their own words to sell them.

Probing discovery questions should be a major part of every sales call you ever make. Finding a way to discuss what your client finds to be a problem and then keeping them talking about it is the bread and butter of daily sales work. It tells you what to sell them, and often how to sell it. Depending on your product or service, you may want to set a minimum number of probing questions for each interaction. I always aim for at least three, even on a grip and grin visit, and there is no upper limit. How does it work in a real-world scenario?

> Let's use the example of a vacuum sales pro. Many questions will talk about the client's problem, and some will try to uncover forgotten needs. "What's the dirtiest area in your house?" "Does anyone in your home have allergies?" "Do you have pets?" "Is mud or sand an issue?" "Do you need to use the vacuum on more than one floor or story?" "Who uses the vacuum at your home?" "Do you vacuum stairs or curtains?" "Will you be vacuuming hard floors, or carpeting, or both?" These are all probing questions that will help the salesperson guide the consumer to the right product, while also reminding the shopper of all the ways they use their vacuum.

Focus on the problem. Every product or service represents a solution to a want or a need. The right probing questions will lead to a sense of urgency on the buyer's part. Most of your probing questions should focus on the pain, or how the solution will be implemented. What problems has the unmet need caused? How it will affect their life or business the longer their need goes unmet? Does this need arise often? How long has it been unmet already? How would it be different if the need were met today?

Focusing on the problem helps you in several ways: you keep the problem front of mind, you develop urgency to resolve the need soon, and you learn as much as possible about the situation. All of this allows you to craft the best possible business case for using your offering.

Sometimes the consumer doesn't know there is a solution available for a need, so they don't mention the need. If our vacuum sales pro doesn't mention the robot vacuum that cleans floors by itself, how many will he sell? If he asks how much time people "waste" vacuuming rooms that could "clean themselves," would he sell more?

It's hard to imagine now, but camera phones didn't catch on right away. When cell phones first started incorporating cameras, shoppers weren't asking about the camera in the phone. Digital photography was new, and there was no Twitter, Instagram, or Facebook. The phones were expensive, and weren't selling well. Then a major cell carrier in my area started using a different discovery process in their sales process. Their salespeople asked shoppers questions like, "Do you ever find yourself wishing you had your camera with you?" and "Do you ever forget to drop off your film to be developed, or worse, forget to pick it up?" A "yes" to either of these questions was a great way to demonstrate the added value of having a phone that had a good digital camera incorporated in it. "What would you take more pictures of if your camera was always with you?" This question made the buyer imagine using the product. "Would you like to see how easy it is to use?" This question led to the shopper trying out the product in the store. The cell carrier went from "we can't unload these things" to having trouble keeping them in stock. The probing discovery questions reminded shoppers of other needs they wanted filled besides a phone.

When you hear another rep or any customer make a pain-focused statement, try to turn it into a question. Develop questions that allow you to explore pain points in a way that your shopper will want to keep talking; sympathize, don't criticize!

Goals – What are your prospect's goals? It doesn't matter if they relate directly to your product at this point. You still need some probing questions that will give you clarity on their goals and plans. Understanding what the prospect is working toward will give you more context for how they will make buying decisions. If your prospect plans to sell their business within 2 years, and your solution will take 3 years to pay for itself, you may not want to emphasize the short-term return on investment. Immediate, short-term, and long-term goals all matter to your current conversation. Equally, they matter to your follow-up visits. Even if your prospect doesn't buy today, you'll have a relevant subject to discuss next time you talk – "how's that goal coming along?" Remembering their goals (make notes!) and supporting them makes you an ally, not just a supplier.

BUILDING VALUE AND URGENCY

A man who dares to waste one hour of time has not discovered the value of life. – Charles Darwin

Just because someone is in the market doesn't mean they are prepared to buy. There are foot-draggers and tire-kickers, window-shoppers and mall-marchers. Even those who intend to make a purchase aren't necessarily sure when they know enough about the subject, or when is the right time to purchase.

Strengthen their urgency to buy. Discussing the problem/need and your relief/solution for it is a very effective method of generating urgency. So is relating your product to the goals of your prospect. But there is another: Excitement!

Selling the Sizzle

A prospect who is not excited is less likely to become a customer. Remember that sales is an art of seduction! You're trying to excite your customer about getting what they want, and encourage them to get it from you. If you're selling cars and saying, "cars are a necessary evil in today's modern world," your chances of making the sale are much lower than if you're talking about, "the seat-of-the-pants thrill of feeling the car accelerate with just a flick of the gas pedal." You need to generate excitement for using the product.

This is the difference between presenting features and benefits and creating urgency for the customer to buy. "Hugging" curves and "mastering" the road are performance characteristics that can be described in boring, clinical terms, or portrayed in exciting, visceral, first person language. Excite them about how the product or service will make them feel! Sensory language will deliver excitement.

Besides choosing language to describe their physical and emotional feelings, describe how the solution will allow a client to meet their goals. Ask them to tell you how they will feel when they have your solution in place – one of your cars in their driveway. The client describing the benefits to themselves is always powerful and motivating.

For shoppers with a strong sense of urgency, it's wise to slow the process down a little, to make sure you have asked all the necessary discovery questions to help them make the best choice. You still need to pinpoint your buyer's needs. If they purchase the wrong solution, even if they were rushing you, the customer will be annoyed.

Let the client sell herself. Sometimes the best probing question is the broadest, because it lets the shopper guide you. "What do you love about watching television?" might be a perfect first question for someone selling cable service. The client's answer will usually lead to the next question. If the shopper likes that it brings the family together for movies, it's time to ask if they'd like to stream content easily.   Then, get back to the pain. "What does it cost to take your family to a movie these days? Or to stream one?" These are questions that will remind your prospect what a great deal streaming movies are. Questioning in the context of the shopper's life maintains their interest, and increases their sense of urgency. An effective sales pro will spend the entire conversation talking about how the shopper uses

TV, and how that can grow. Then the shopper will sell themselves.

Avoid asking yes or no questions. Those questions box you in, and slow conversations down to a grinding halt. Ex: "Are you looking for a wireless solution?" A question with a one-word answer makes the customer feel less included in the process, because they don't have the opportunity to express themselves. It stops urgency and interest in its tracks. Remember, people love to talk about themselves!

Keep your shoppers talking! Have a long list of solid questions. They keep the conversation going. Ex: "If this product were completely perfect and free, what would it do for you?" Ask anything that gets the shopper to talk about their ideal solution. "Tell me about the product you're replacing. Why are you in the market?" There will be useful information in the answer! When you use these questions, you'll be learning what your client's ideal solution is. Your response might start with, "Let's get as close to that ideal as we can."

Think about it now. What are some questions that will help you and your prospect both focusing on what they need? What questions will help bring up their sense of urgency? What specific language will build excitement, and make your customer crave the satisfaction of owning your product? List at least five, and aim for ten. Memorize them over time. These will be key to every call you make. Every time you think of another one, write it down, and add it to your list. Soon you will have developed a powerful list of questions to develop urgency.

Building Value

As your you walk through the conversation that builds their urgency, your prospect will be telling you what they value in the potential purchase they may make. You may mention a feature, and they may completely ignore it. Okay, they didn't value that one. You may ask if they're looking for a different feature, and they may light up like the Vegas strip. Pay dirt! Your job is to listen, and repeat what they value in the context of your offering. Simultaneously, gently remind them of the discomfort of living without those things that they value.

Going back to the car analogy, whatever they have told you up to now tells you what they value. Repeat it back to them. "So, with this new Mercedes in the driveway, you'll be looking forward to the daily commute, you won't be worrying about whether it's going to break down when your daughter takes it to visit her brother at college, and it just might annoy the heck out of that guy across the street!"

Sometimes the material they give you will be better than others, and you may need to add a couple of values of your own. But they key here is to focus on what they value. If they don't value that alloy wheels are standard, or that you've won 12 JD Power awards in the last 3 years, don't talk about it, or don't talk about it much. No one wants to be sold – everyone wants to buy. Talking about what they don't value will cause them to lose interest quickly.

If your product requires a presentation and/or a proposal, guess what? Yep, that's right. You'll write your presentation or proposal with more emphasis on what they value, and less on what didn't excite them. If you do this, they'll pay attention from beginning to end. If you don't, they won't be interested because they'll feel misunderstood.

OVERCOMING OBJECTIONS

Objections in sales are a good thing. It means the buyer has begun qualifying you. – Elisabeth Marino

It would be wonderful if prospects and buyers told us everything we need to know, believed exactly what we told them, and bought what they needed in a timely manner. It's rarely that easy. Like all people, buyers forget things, get busy, get confused, have doubts, work with budgets, and make bad decisions. All these human foibles present themselves in the sales process in the form of objections.

Objections

An objection is anything the prospective buyer does or says to slow or stop the buying process. They fall into three categories: real, partially real, and fake.

There are only four real objections: no need, no interest, no money, and no belief in your brand or offering. Those are the only things that mean it's not likely to be worth a sales conversation currently. It may be worth some networking and discovery, but it's not going to end up in your pipeline until one or more of these issues are resolved.

Fake objections, on the other hand, are almost incalculable in number! "I don't have time." "I'll need to talk to my boss about this." "Send me something in writing. If I'm interested, I'll respond." "We've decided to delay this project." "I've never heard of you/your company." And on, and on, and on.

What's a partially real objection? It's an objection in which the buyer thinks there's a problem you can't solve for them, and the concern is based in some reality. They may be afraid of hearing the bad news, so they cut you off in advance: "I'm sure you're way out of our price point." "We need it next week, and you can't do that, can you?" "We never pay extra for a service contract, so you're out of the running." "Well, my wife/partner really likes company B, so this is a waste of time." "I saw a news story about your industry, and I don't think I want to get involved."

Responding to a "Fake" Objection?

It depends on when it's offered. If it's offered while you're trying to set an appointment, it usually means, "I don't have time or interest in having this conversation right now." So respect that, and reach out again later.

But when it's offered during the sales process, it means something completely different. It means the buyer has begun qualifying you and your offering. "I can't afford that right now," may mean they are unaware of available credit terms, or they assume the price is higher than it is. Or, they may not have calculated the true cost of their need, and don't see how quick the return on investment really is.

Whatever the case, the objection that comes during the sales process is the buyer's way to re-focus the conversation on their concerns. If they are price-sensitive, that's where they'll go. If they are change-resistant, they'll talk about their relationship with their current provider. If they are worried about service, they'll say something like, "And when it all goes wrong, where will you guys be? Nowhere to be found, just like the last guy..."

When these objections come up, you need to avoid looking at them as negatives, and instead look at them as an invitation to present another strength, feature, or benefit. I recommend asking a question or two about the objection first, to ensure that you're responding to their real concern.

"Has that happened to you before?" "What kind of pricing problem do you anticipate?" "What makes you say that?" and other questions encourage the prospect to tell their story and get their concern out into the open. Then offer, "I'm sorry to hear that happened. That would upset me, too."

After the story is out, you can relay to them why their issue is a value to you or your company, and how it can be avoided. It's much easier to put their mind at rest when you know the whole story, so make sure you find a way to get them to share it. They'll feel better, and you're more likely to make a sale.

Partially Real Objections

Each of these is a real concern based on some fact, but it doesn't mean the conversation needs to end. These objections are ideal opportunities to educate your prospect as to what is and isn't relevant to their buying process. Additionally, it's an opening discuss any customizations you're willing or able to make, ask for a meeting with the rest of the decision makers, or learn more about their needs.

What's important is that you just take the objection and face calmly, head on.

"We want your business. What price are you worried about? Is it price or terms that concern you?"

"We are very responsive to your timeline. What day and time, specifically, do you need the solution in place?"

"Our service contract comes with the purchase, so the number I'll be quoting you is the total price."

"We value strong partnerships. What is it about company B that makes your wife/partner so loyal?"

"I saw that same story. If you're not familiar with the specifics, it makes sense that you're concerned. Let me walk you through it."

An Ounce of Prevention…

Preventing objections is always a great way to ensure the conversation is focused on real values and concerns, but how do you do it?

Buyers often have misconceptions about the product, the buying process, the implementation, or the governing laws related to a purchase. Remember, they aren't specialists in the field like you are! No matter how wrong these preconceptions are, they are very likely to be a factor in the buying process.

When there are common objections based on misconceptions, I like to flatter my prospect a little bit, and diffuse the objection at the same time. I mention the objection before they can. "Well, you seem to have done your homework, so you know that XYZ is a common misconception. It's a relief that you're so knowledgeable in this area." No matter what they say next, I'm in the position of expert in the field. If they didn't know, they may ask about it, and we get it out of the way early. If they did know, they feel like I understand them.

When there are common objections that are based in some reality, like a negative article the buyer may have read, or a competitor's bad business practice, again, prevention is your friend. Just bring it up early in the conversation.

"I've heard from some of my customers that they thought XYZ. Is that something you're concerned about?" "I'm really glad you said something, so we can talk about it now."

The most important thing to do with an objection is to get to the bottom of it. The prospective buyer brought it up for a reason – it's important to them. Worst case scenario? They're right, and you can't move forward now. Better to learn that early, before you waste a lot of everyone's time and energy. Best case scenario? You learn more about the buyer and their values, which allows you to present your offer in its best possible light.

Keep track of the most common objections you hear. If you work with other sales reps, try to keep track of the ones they hear, too. Write up a list of the top 5-10, and effective responses to them. Practice those responses until they're smooth. Don't let objections derail another sales call!

CLOSING THE SALE

Don't celebrate closing the sale, celebrate opening a relationship. –
Patricia Fripp

A t last! You're at the closing stage! You've done your discovery, proven value, overcome objections, provided a proposal, and aligned the prospect's needs with your offer. It's time to get the signature. Woo hoo! Finally!

Slow down, there, Sparky. Don't count your chickens before they are hatched. Savvy buyers will often make their strongest negotiation arguments during the closing meeting. And you, the seller, can't be left flat footed.

Asking for the Sale

Strange, but true, many sales reps never ask for the sale. In fact, they go out of their way to avoid it for fear of being perceived as "pushy." That's just silly!

Your buyer knows they are in a conversation about buying something. They expect to buy something. And a significant number of buyers don't know that it's time to move the relationship forward and buy something. They will stay in "research" mode for as long as you let them. It's your responsibility to let them know that it's time to move forward.

We will be covering a few of the most common ways to ask for the sale here. Some come right out and say, "Do we have a deal?" while others are a little more subtle, but all of them make it clear that it's time to take the business relationship to one of supplier and client. After we discuss the closing techniques, we'll go over some of the last-minute negotiations you may face.

The easiest close out there is, **"I think it's time to move forward."** They will disagree with you, and you'll go back to discussing value and building urgency. OR They will agree with you, and you take the next step. It's very straightforward. And if you've positioned yourself as the expert, it's clear that you'll know when it's time to make the deal.

The **"assumptive"** close is when you assume that they are already a customer, and start asking ownership questions like, "when would you like to take delivery?" Or "You can pick this up tomorrow after 12 noon." If you've proven value and developed urgency, it works well. However, some buyers are offended by this close, and feel railroaded and disrespected. If this happens, apologize for the misunderstanding immediately, and ask them what else they'd like to discuss.

The **"A or B"** close is a variation of the assumptive close. You have narrowed the buyer's preferences down to two clear choices, and you ask them to choose one. "Are we going with the stainless steel, or the matte black?" "Will that be pick up or delivery?" Once that decision is made, you move forward as if they have agreed to the purchase.

The **"which option"** close is another variation of the assumptive close, and it's used when there are many details to a purchase. "Will we be needing the air conditioning? Tinted windows? Power seats? Keyless entry?" As you go down the list, you are building a specific package for the customer. Once the package is complete, you provide the price and the agreement.

The **"takeaway"** close often feels cheesy, and I recommend you use it only when it's completely true. The basis here is that the offer is only available for a limited time. If you're selling pies, and you only have one left, it makes sense to mention it. "Shop now! Supply is limited!" A "limited time" offer is very easy to verify, and most buyers feel like it's a pressure tactic. Use it sparingly.

The **"U-turn"** close is good for buyers who ask for extras at the last minute. "We need you to throw in the service contract at no additional cost." The close on this, if you have management approval, is, "If I can do that for you, do you commit to making the deal today? Because I think I can get my manager to agree to that." The buyer doesn't expect you to agree, or to have to commit right now, so they are usually surprised. If they are serious about moving forward, they will agree.

The **"sandwich"** close is good when you have to say "no" to something on the prospect's wish list. You sandwich the bad news between two pieces of good news. "We've agreed on the turbo model. We don't have the silver in stock, but we have the light grey. We have the options package that you like, and it's being prepped for delivery right now." If the prospect doesn't accept this offer, often you can get them to commit to the purchase of what they want, and then place an order to meet their exact wish list.

The Last-Minute Buyer Ask

Sales is not for the cowardly, and this is a classic reason why. You've gotten all the way to the closing, and the buyer comes up with a request that hasn't been discussed or agreed on before. Now what?

This is a classic move for savvy buyers. They'll ask for an add-on, or a change in terms that makes things more favorable to them at the last minute because they know the seller has invested a lot of time and effort in the sales process. And often, they are right. The seller is willing to make certain concessions to get the deal closed.

Watch out! This is dangerous territory. Don't agree to anything right away. Let the request hang in the air. Often after a few seconds, the buyer will back track with a remark like, "Well, I had to try."

If they don't, you can't give in without losing credibility. You've told them the price. The price is the price. Any deviation makes it look as if you're gouging. The way around this is to "Talk to" your manager. Go for a U-turn close (see above.) Then, even if it's a charade, go through with talking to your manager. Then make it clear to the buyer that the concession was hard-won, and there won't be any more concessions. It's time to make the purchase.

If the buyer's "ask" is ridiculous, and sometimes it is, go back to your discovery skills. "I don't think I understand. Can you walk me through how we got here?" and "Tell me more about that." You'll go back to overcoming objections, and providing a clearer understanding of the value of your product. Sometimes they won't relent. And in that case, you need to walk away. Disengage nicely but firmly. "I'm sorry we couldn't meet your terms. Best of luck on your project."

The Agreement

Setting reasonable expectations for what ownership or a purchase will mean is key to getting the signature, but what's key to a sale staying closed is that the buyer understands exactly what they are buying.

Most of us have a variety of offerings, services, options, and price points. It's not uncommon for a buyer to think they are buying everything they liked about every package, not just what is included in the one they have chosen. That's a big letdown for them to accept when they realize what they really purchased.

A good place to start is what needs to be on a credit card receipt. A credit card receipt needs to list the buyer, the seller, the specific goods or services sold, the price paid, the date of the transaction, and a traceable transaction ID number. That's a great list to include in your closing cycle. All those things need to be discussed to ensure clarity on the part of the buyer.

If there are things that were attractive to your buyer that are not included, make sure they understand that they did not choose that option. The specifics of the purchase, all of them, need to be listed somewhere in the agreement. Go over them with your buyer specifically. I usually do this by saying, "Let's make sure we didn't overlook anything. Let's go over these details one more time."

If, after reviewing the details, the prospect asks for a lower price, don't

Elisabeth Marino

do it! Instead, ask them what they would like to remove from the deal to achieve the price they want. "You'd like 20% off? Then we can remove the service agreement to get to that price. Will that work for you?" Don't backpedal on the price. It devalues your product!

FOLLOW-UP

You didn't come this far to stop or turn around. – Elisabeth Marino

There are two kinds of follow-up: follow-up to land a client, and follow-up to keep a client. Successful sales reps are experts at both. Let's start with follow-up to land a client.

Following Up with Prospects

The process of identifying your prospects takes time. And if that prospect is truly a potential client, don't let the lack of a few phone calls keep you from winning the deal.

The statistics on follow-up calls change constantly, and not in your favor. Most sales take a minimum of 5 attempts at an initial engagement, but the average (as of this writing) is 13! People are just harder to reach than ever before. And more people and things are vying for their attention. In order to make appointments, you need to keep prospecting consistently.

I could go on and on about not getting discouraged, but it won't help. Either you like prospecting or you don't, but it's irrelevant. To be successful in sales, you have to do it. Prospecting is largely a numbers game. It's that simple. If you give up before you reach someone, or before you can thoroughly qualify them as a potential buyer, who decided they won't buy from you? *You did!* What a silly decision that is...

Getting to talk to someone doesn't mean you'll be able to schedule an appointment. Scheduling an appointment doesn't mean they will keep it. If they keep it, that doesn't mean they'll be in the market right now. But the only way that all your effort was wasted is if you choose to disengage. The buyer is under no obligation to find you. It's your job to find them, make a great impression, and be there to help guide their purchasing decision when the time is right. They may not make it easy for you, but it's part of the job.

Use everything in your arsenal to follow up. Email, door knocks, LinkedIn, social media, phone calls, and networking events all can help you establish contact. Try reaching out every 4 or 5 business days. More often is pushy. Less often is forgettable.

Following Up with Clients

Following up with clients begins during the sale. At the closing, clarify with your customer what the next steps will be, who will take them, and how everyone involved can contact each other.

Most sales are the most vulnerable to problems in the first few days to few weeks after the sale. (Or, if delivery isn't immediate, the time between signature and delivery.) "Buyer's remorse" sometimes sets in, and any doubts or concerns the buyer may have had begun to fester. It's vital that someone do a little handholding to make sure that their concerns are resolved before they grow out of control.

If you are the account manager, give them another card, and confirm who the primary point of contact will be on their end. Make it clear when the next step will occur, and what it will be.

In many cases, sales reps hand off a closed account to customer service. If possible, provide your customer with the name and contact information of the specific rep who will be assigned to their account. Give them an idea of when to expect an onboarding call, and determine who the primary account contact on the client side should be. After the closing, send an introductory email to both the client contact and the customer service rep putting them in direct contact.

When it isn't possible to give them a specific name and contact information, supply them with the customer care line and any other information they will need to follow-up on their purchase. Encourage them to reach out to you directly if they need to navigate any other relationships with your company. Don't leave the impression that now that you have their money you no longer care. It will always come back to bite you!

The day after you close, send a quick hand-written thank you note to your buyer (not only an email.) Enclose your card, and a short personal note. Most companies and sales reps don't do it, and clients respect it. It goes a long way to dispelling buyer concerns, and strengthens the new relationship.

If you haven't done so already, request a connection on LinkedIn with your client. Like and share their content. Make it clear that your interest in them is ongoing. It will help them keep you top-of-mind when it comes time to make referrals to you and your business.

EPILOGUE

Key Habits of Elite-Level Sales Pros

After working with sales reps in over a hundred companies in over 40 industries, I've noticed that the very top reps have quite a few of the same habits. I started asking these high-performing reps just what they do that drives them to consistently achieve at a higher level. Here are the answers. How many of these habits do you have?

Continuous Professional Development

They train their strengths and weaknesses. They read, attend conferences and workshops, and network with mentors who can help them improve. They don't just focus on the parts of the job they like; they work to improve all their skills.

Every sales rep has strengths and weaknesses, but most set goals based on avoiding their weaknesses. If they don't prospect well, they'll set their goals based on proposals or average ticket, as an example.

High-performing reps train their weaknesses to build them up. But they also get creative. A high-performance rep who doesn't prospect well might focus more effort on gaining referrals, or maintaining an active business network to keep the leads rolling in. They'll apply the same amount of time to traditional prospecting, and work on honing those skills, but they'll find a way to guarantee success as they work toward better prospecting proficiency.

Focusing on weakness is no one's favorite activity. Working on a plan to ensure greater success is energizing!

They Use Their CRM Thoroughly

Although some of the top reps I work with have a love/hate relationship with their CRM, none of them want to give it up! Unanimously the complaint is that it takes a lot of time to accurately note all the appropriate and applicable data. But every rep who said this was clear on the value of the dashboard data to themselves and to management. They use the data every day, and would hate to have to do all of it by hand in a notebook.

CRMs help reps keep track of the strength of their pipeline, track activity levels, concentrate and categorize relevant account and prospect data, make calls, send emails, manage their calendar, and much more. Top reps develop ways for their CRMs to save them time and boost their performance.

They Consistently Use a Set Sales Process

Top reps design their goals based on what they can control. Setting results-based goals can sometimes be dangerous. Top reps know they can't control the availability or mood of those they call on, the weather, or a client's cash flow. What they can control is their own actions. Having a clear and consistent sales process makes sure they're doing all they can do to keep the sale on track.

Pacing a sale makes a huge difference is average ticket and customer experience. Sales processes are developed and honed to pace a sale well, and have specific goals for each step. When the goals are achieved, the next step is scheduled. This keeps seller organized and buyers from becoming overwhelmed. It lays a strong foundation for qualified sales.

A defined process also allows reps to diagnose their own trouble spots as they arise. If deals are most often breaking down at the proposal stage, they'll make it their goal to complete a more thorough discovery stage and write stronger proposal. They'll ask some different questions, or do a deeper dive on the ones they're currently asking.

They Set Individual Goals

Sales pros who consistently crush quota set their own goals to make it happen. Rather than rely on the corporate KPIs like dials and door knocks, they make their own list of the activities and levels they need to excel. They often include activities that management doesn't insist on, like networking time, or thank you notes. In their one-on-ones with management, they'll bring their own activity tracker in and discuss the challenges they've identified. They'll role-play parts of the sales process that aren't going smoothly. They are always looking to improve.

High-performing reps know sharing personal goals with managers is motivating. Their managers become co-conspirators; everybody wants the moonshot to succeed! Support is consistent, and managers regularly invest in their success.

It's not that they ignore the preset "plan" goals – they are just self-aware enough to know what activities push them well past quota. "Plan" goals aren't always motivating to them, so they identify what is. Top sales reps are not happy with the middle of the pack; they aim for President's Club or Winner's Circle or Elite status. They look at their jobs as the series of tasks that bring them to the signature on the agreement. Anything that slows that down is avoided at all costs.

They're Team Players

Top sales pros are acutely aware that sales is a team sport. These reps ask everyone for help, and they give assistance freely when asked. They are team players within their companies and with their clients.

When they talk to a buyer, they say things like, "Help me understand your process." And, "How can I learn more about this?" They know that they don't know everything, and they don't reinvent the wheel. They love to learn about and from their buyers.

Likewise, when they're stuck on any part of their process or new products, they lean on management for training and printed material to get a clear understanding. They know that the best way to become a better rep is to develop their knowledge and skills.

They share their knowledge and their effort with teammates whenever they can reasonably do so. Relying on each other for knowledge or help reaching a deadline is part of what makes teams strong.

They Walk Away From Dead Deals

Really. They don't get emotionally attached to their prospect list. Walking away from a dead deal early is a tough habit to create, but it saves tons of time and energy! Once they've developed the habit, their stress levels go way down. Among other things, they avoid developing bad habits like selling on price, or negotiating value instead of demonstrating it. If the prospect won't engage on needs and value, they move on.

Multiple studies have demonstrated that reps spend more than twice as much time on deals that don't close than on deals that do. By walking away, high performing reps can focus on other deals that have a better likelihood of closing, and forecast sales more accurately.

Why is it so hard for most of us to walk away? 1) We're sure we can meet the client's needs, and are sure they are about to realize it. 2) We know it can be tough to find a strong lead to replace this one.

What makes it easy for Rockstar reps to walk away? 1) The customer knows how to find them. If the rep has proven value, the buyer will call when they're ready. 2) They have a solid pipeline and a bank of qualified prospects, so they move on to the next one. 3) Top reps have a strong follow-up calendar, and they'll keep in limited touch. 4) They realize the sale isn't about them at all. It's about what's going on with the customer. Sometimes customers are going to make a bad choice. Top sales don't take it personally.

Cultivate these habits, and the skills you've found throughout this book. You'll be a better sales professional, and you'll close more business because of it. Best wishes, and stay dynamic!

-    Elisabeth Marino

Elisabeth Marino

If you enjoyed this book, please join my mailing list to be notified of additional titles and upcoming events. Click here: http://salesdynamoconsulting.com/contact-us/

www.ingramcontent.com/pod-product-compliance
Lightning Source LLC
Chambersburg PA
CBHW021504210526
45463CB00002B/879